MY COMMUNITY

A TRIP TO THE TOWN HALL

Gloria Santos

PowerKiDS press.

New York

Published in 2017 by The Rosen Publishing Group, Inc.
29 East 21st Street, New York, NY 10010

First Edition

Editor: Melissa Raé Shofner
Book Design: Mickey Harmon

Photo Credits: Cover theboone/Getty Images; p. 5 THOMAS COEX/Getty Images; p. 6 Alistair Berg/Getty Images; p. 9 Monty Rakusen/Getty Images; p. 10 Susan Chiang/Getty Images; p. 13 Blend Images - Hill Street Studios/Getty Images; p. 14 heshphoto/Getty Images; p. 17 Rawpixel.com/Shutterstock.com; p. 18 Brand New Images/Getty Images; p. 21Caiaimage/Sam Edwards/Getty Images; p. 22 Joseph Sohm/Shutterstock.com.

Cataloging-In-Publication Data

Names: Santos, Gloria.
Title: A trip to the town hall / Gloria Santos.
Description: New York : PowerKids Press, 2017. | Series: My community | Includes index.
Identifiers: ISBN 9781499427776 (pbk.) | ISBN 9781499430103 (library bound) | ISBN 9781508152965 (6 pack)
Subjects: LCSH: Local government--United States--Juvenile literature.
Classification: LCC JS331.S26 2017 | DDC 320.8'50973--d23

Manufactured in the United States of America

CPSIA Compliance Information: Batch #BW17PK: For Further Information contact Rosen Publishing, New York, New York at 1-800-237-9932

CONTENTS

The **town hall** is busy.

Town leaders work there.

Town leaders make laws.

IN THE BEST LOCATION

STOP

Laws keep **people** safe.

The town hall helps people.

BULLETIN BOARD
RULES
SUMMER
SATURDAYS

People can find jobs.

There are town meetings.

TOWN PLAN
Public Library (in the future)
Pool
Office
Co-working Room
Backyard Garden with Trees
Private Working Space
Extra space for activities
Living & Dining Room
Bathroom & Toilet
Concrete
Grass
Wooden Floor
Acrylic Floor
HNTB
Veniam

People ask about the town.

People can share news.

TOWN HALL

Every town needs a town hall.

WORDS TO KNOW

people

town hall

town leaders

INDEX

WEBSITES

Due to the changing nature of Internet links, PowerKids Press has developed an online list of websites related to the subject of this book. This site is updated regularly. Please use this link to access the list: www.powerkidslinks.com/mycom/townhall